# Crayola™

# COOKING
## with Color

# Crayola™
# COOKING
## with Color

INSIGHT
EDITIONS

SAN RAFAEL • LOS ANGELES • LONDON

# CONTENTS

# INTRODUCTION

Cooking and creating are two of the most rewarding and fun activities a family can do together. Crayola® *Cooking with Color* features 40 recipes for every meal of the day—breakfast, lunch, dinner, snack time, and dessert—that highlight foods in colors across the color wheel.

The recipes are inspired by the names of actual Crayola crayons. Check out the Yummy Yellow chapter for **Sunny Side Up** Egg Cups (page 17) and **Unmellow Yellow** Pineapple-Fried Rice (page 21). Start the day with a **Razzmatazz** Raspberry Smoothie (page 33) for breakfast and end it with **Pinky Pink** Shrimp Tacos (page 38) for dinner from Totally Rad Red and Pink. Take **Twist O' Lime** Guacamole (page 94) to a party, and whip up a batch of **Blue Blazes** Nachos (page 70) made with blue corn tortilla chips and refried black beans for lunch.

Throughout the book, you'll find suggestions for pairing vibrantly colored foods to create edible art and good nutrition (see "Make a Color Poppin' Plate!"). Try **Macaroni & Cheese** Mac & Cheese (page 52) with gorgeous green steamed broccoli, a **B'Dazzled Blue** Butterfly Pea Flower Tea Latte (page 81) with bright and juicy orange segments, or **Glowing Green** Avocado Toast (page 86) with sweet and succulent purple grapes.

In between chapters there is a Crayola craft project that will add to the fun of cooking and sitting down together to eat what you've made. Spiff up your table with a Tie Dye Coffee Filter Flowers Centerpiece (page 46) or a Melted Crayon Confetti Lantern (page 29)—or make movie night extra-special with Family Movie Night Snack Holders (page 64).

Cooking together as a family makes eating—something we all have to do several times every day—an opportunity for trying a new taste, learning a new skill, or simply spending time together. Look for steps in the recipes labeled "Kids Can Help!" for safe and smart ways to get everyone involved and "Adult Helper" for those steps in the craft projects that require adult supervision.

Creating a colorful plate and table adds fun to mealtime and fuels active bodies with healthful foods the whole family will love.

# COLOR, COOK, CREATE!

## Kids Can Help!

Before you start cooking, there are a few things that everyone in the family should keep in mind:

**Read through the recipe:** Start at the beginning and read all of the way to the end. If you don't understand exactly what to do in every step, ask a grown-up helper to read through the recipe with you.

**Check the ingredients:** Read through the ingredient list and make sure you have everything you need.

**Go step-by-step:** Finish each step of the recipe before you move on to the next one.

**Clean up:** When you are done cooking, clean up. Wash and dry the pots and pans and dishes you used, or put them in the dishwasher. Fill the sink with hot, soapy water and wipe down the counters. Put everything away.

**Be safe:** Although it's a blast for kids to stir, whisk, plop, drop, and roll their way through the kitchen, there should always be an adult helper supervising because injuries and accidents can happen where there are knives and other sharp objects, heat sources, and electric appliances. And while everybody can get involved in the fun, there are tasks that are appropriate for different ages.

- **Toddlers (ages 2-3):** Even the littlest cooks can measure liquid and dry ingredients with measuring cups and spoons, stir (away from the stove), and sprinkle on fresh herbs or cheese.

- **Preschoolers (ages 4-5):** Kids in this age group can wash produce, pick the leaves off of herbs, whisk eggs, mash potatoes or avocados with a potato masher, and roll dough.

- **School-age (ages 6-7):** These budding chefs are ready to crack and separate eggs, peel fruits and vegetables, grate cheese and citrus, set the table, and help with the dishes.

- **Culinary kids (ages 8+):** After a few years of experience under their apron strings, these junior chefs are ready to read through a recipe, help with meal planning, help with a grocery list, use kid-safe knives, bake simple recipes such as quick breads and cookies, and do some simple sautéing on the stove.

# Food and Kitchen Safety

Raw foods and unwashed fruits and vegetables can contain bacteria that can make you sick if you don't treat them properly. Follow this food safety checklist:

● Always wash your hands before you start cooking. Wash them again after handling raw meat, poultry, or fish.

● Before using fresh fruits and vegetables, wash them under cool running water.

● Use separate cutting boards for raw meats and vegetables, and always clean the cutting boards right after use.

● Don't eat raw eggs or meat—and don't put cooked food on a plate that had raw food on it. Don't eat foods that have raw eggs in them (like cookie dough!).

● Every recipe tells you when your food is done cooking. Cook it until it's done.

● If you are thawing food that is frozen, thaw it in the refrigerator overnight. Never thaw foods on the counter.

The kitchen is one of the most fun rooms in the house, but grown-ups should help teach kids the proper use and safety of cooking tools. Follow this kitchen safety checklist:

● Always have a grown-up show kids how to use kitchen tools safely.

● Tie back your hair, if necessary. Roll up your sleeves, and take off any loose clothing that might get in the way.

● Pick up knives and kitchen scissors by the handle. Never put them in a sink full of water. They are hard to see, and if you reach into the water, you might get hurt. Have a grown-up show kids how to use them safely.

● Always use hot pads to remove things from the oven, stove top, or microwave; never use a kitchen towel.

● Steam is very hot and can burn. When foods cook, steam builds up under pan lids and foil-covered pans. To uncover a pan full of food that has been cooking, lift the edge of the cover that is farthest away from you.

● Keep electric appliances such as toasters, blenders, and electric mixers far away from the sink and stove. Water and electricity don't mix, and cords can melt on a hot burner.

● As soon as you are done with an electric appliance, unplug it. Check that the oven and burners are off, too.

● Clean as you cook. Wipe up spills and messes to keep from slipping and falling. Keep the counter clean.

# Yummy YELLOW

Brilliant, eye-catching yellow is all around us, from warm sunshine to the sturdy school bus to a field of daffodils. The fresh fruits and vivid vegetables in this chapter—bananas, sweet peppers, pineapples, lemons, and corn—contain nutrients like potassium, which is good for the heart, kidneys, and bones, and vitamin C to boost immunity. These recipes will brighten your table and the rest of your day.

# SUNNY SIDE UP EGG CUPS

Start your day on the bright side with these cheesy, veggie-flecked mini frittatas made in muffin cups. Pair with **Blue Berry Blue** Muffins (page 69) or **Mini Brown** Bran Muffins (page 105) for a matching meal that can be enjoyed at home or on the go. (It's perfectly acceptable to eat them with your hands!)

Leftovers can be stored in the refrigerator for up to three days. Let them cool completely, store in a sealed container or wrapped in plastic, and reheat in the microwave for 30 seconds at a time until heated through (1 to 1½ minutes). Let stand for a minute or two before eating.

**ACTIVE TIME: 20 MINUTES**
**TOTAL TIME: 40 MINUTES**
**MAKES 6 SERVINGS (2 EGG CUPS EACH)**

|   | |
|---|---|
| | Olive oil cooking spray for coating |
| 1 | tablespoon olive oil |
| ¼ | cup finely chopped yellow bell pepper |
| ¼ | cup finely chopped orange bell pepper |
| 1 | green onion, thinly sliced (white and green parts) |
| 6 | eggs |
| ½ | cup milk |
| ¼ | teaspoon salt |
| ⅛ | teaspoon ground black pepper |
| 1 | cup shredded Cheddar cheese |
| ¾ | cup finely cubed ham (optional) |
| | Grape tomatoes, halved, and chopped fresh parsley, for garnish (optional) |

Heat oven to 350°F. Coat 12 standard-size muffin cups with olive oil cooking spray.

Heat olive oil in a skillet over medium heat. Add the bell peppers and onion. Cook, stirring frequently, until vegetables are softened, 5 to 7 minutes. Remove from heat.

**KIDS CAN HELP!** In a medium bowl, whisk together the eggs, milk, salt, and black pepper. Slowly stir the cooked vegetables, cheese, and ham, if using, into the egg mixture. Divide evenly among the muffin cups.

Bake until frittatas are set in the middle and lightly browned, about 20 minutes.

Garnish with tomatoes and parley, if desired.

**Make a Color Poppin' Plate!** Serve with a side of red grapes and green avocado, sliced or on toast.

# LIQUID GOLD CREAMY CORN CHOWDER

Two kinds of cheese, bacon, and a bag of frozen diced potatoes with peppers and onions bring the Midas touch to this simple and satisfying chowder. Try it with a dash of hot sauce to give it a kick!

ACTIVE TIME: 30 MINUTES
TOTAL TIME: 30 MINUTES
MAKES 6 SERVINGS

- 4 slices bacon, chopped
- ¼ cup butter
- 1 (28-ounce) bag frozen diced potatoes with peppers and onions
- 2 cups frozen corn kernels
- 1 (15-ounce) can creamed corn
- 2 cups low-sodium chicken broth
- 1 (8-ounce) package cream cheese or light cream cheese (neufchâtel), cubed and at room temperature
- 2 cups shredded Cheddar cheese
- ½ teaspoon salt
- ¼ teaspoon ground black pepper

  Sliced green onions, for garnish (optional)

In a large soup pot, cook the bacon over medium heat until browned and crisp, 6 to 8 minutes. Using a slotted spoon, transfer the bacon to a paper towel-lined plate to drain.

Add the butter to the pot and let it melt. Add the potatoes and cook, stirring occasionally, until very lightly browned, about 6 minutes.

Stir in the frozen corn, creamed corn, and broth. Bring to a boil. Reduce heat to a simmer and cook until potatoes are tender, about 5 minutes. Stir in cream cheese.

**KIDS CAN HELP!** Reduce heat to low and add the shredded cheese in handfuls, stirring after each addition, until melted and creamy.

Season the chowder with salt and pepper.

**KIDS CAN HELP!** Top each serving with the crisp-cooked bacon. Garnish with sliced green onions, if desired.

**Make a Color Poppin' Plate!** Serve with sliced carrots and bell peppers with a side of hummus or dipping sauce.

# UNMELLOW YELLOW
## PINEAPPLE FRIED RICE

Packed with flavor from ginger, garlic, soy, chicken apple sausage, a hit of rice vinegar—and sweetness from fresh pineapple—this golden Thai-style stir-fry will put energizing yellow front and center at dinnertime.

ACTIVE TIME: 30 MINUTES
TOTAL TIME: 30 MINUTES
MAKES 4 SERVINGS

- 2 tablespoons peanut oil
- 2 links chicken apple sausage, thinly sliced on the diagonal
- 1 large clove garlic, minced
- 2 teaspoons grated fresh ginger root
- ½ small sweet onion, chopped
- 1 small yellow bell pepper, stemmed, seeded, and chopped
- 1½ cups diced pineapple, fresh or canned in juice or water, drained
- 1 tablespoon soy sauce
- 1 tablespoon rice vinegar
- ½ teaspoon ground white pepper
  Salt
- 4 cups cooked rice*
- 2 green onions, thinly sliced, and fresh pineapple wedges, for garnish (optional)

In a large nonstick skillet, heat 1 tablespoon of peanut oil over medium-high. Cook the sausage slices until browned and crisp on the edges, 6 to 8 minutes, stirring frequently. Remove the sausage from the pan and set aside.

Add the remaining 1 tablespoon of peanut oil to the skillet and reduce heat to medium. Add the garlic and ginger and stir to combine. Keep stirring until fragrant, about 1 minute. Add the onion and cook, stirring frequently, until translucent, 3 to 4 minutes. Add the bell pepper and cook until softened slightly, about 3 minutes. Add the pineapple and cook for another 2 minutes while stirring frequently. Add soy sauce, vinegar, white pepper, and salt to taste. Stir to combine.

Turn heat to medium-high. Add rice and cook, stirring constantly until rice is heated through and all ingredients are well combined. Add the cooked sausage and stir again until evenly incorporated.

**KIDS CAN HELP!** Transfer to a serving platter. Garnish with green onions and pineapple wedges, if desired, and serve immediately.

**\*Tip:** For best results, use day-old rice that has been chilled in the refrigerator. The grains will separate much more easily than just-cooked rice, which sticks together.

# SHOOTING STAR BITES

For a snack that will shoot your taste buds into the stratosphere, buttery crackers topped with ranch cream cheese and twinkling yellow pepper stars shine equally bright at a weekday afternoon playdate or party spread. For an all-you-can-nibble buffet, serve these with **Neon Carrot** Hummus (page 59) and **Piggy Pink** Pinwheels (page 41), with **Little Lemon** Bars (page 25) or **Kiwi**-Key Lime Tartlets (page 97) for dessert.

ACTIVE TIME: 30 MINUTES
TOTAL TIME: 30 MINUTES
MAKES 32 BITES

- 1 (8-ounce) package cream cheese or light cream cheese (neufchâtel), softened
- 2 tablespoons whole milk
- ½ packet ranch dressing and dip mix
- 1 cup finely shredded Cheddar cheese
- 4 large yellow bell peppers
- 32 rich round crackers
  Star-shape cookie cutter, 1½ to 2 inches
- 96 1-inch chive pieces

**KIDS CAN HELP!** In a small bowl, combine the cream cheese and milk. Beat vigorously with a wooden spoon until creamy and fluffy. Add the ranch dressing mix and stir until well combined. Add the shredded cheese and stir until well combined.

Place one pepper on a cutting board stem side up. Cut off each of the four "cheeks" of the pepper. Discard the stem and seeds. Repeat with the remaining peppers.

**KIDS CAN HELP!** Use the cookie cutter to make star-shape pepper pieces. Spread each cracker with about 1 tablespoon of the cream cheese spread. Top with a yellow pepper star, skin side up, and 3 chive pieces. Arrange on a serving platter.

**Make a Color Poppin' Plate!** Serve with **Caribbean Sea** Coolers (page 98).

# LITTLE LEMON BARS

The rich, buttery shortbread crust perfectly balances out the sweet-yet-tart lemon filling in these petite treats. The best news? They're small—so you can have more than one!

ACTIVE TIME: 30 MINUTES
TOTAL TIME: 45 MINUTES +
COOLING AND CHILLING
MAKES 54 BARS

**FOR THE CRUST**

- ½ cup (1 stick) butter, melted
- ¼ cup granulated sugar
- 1 teaspoon vanilla extract
- ¼ teaspoon salt
- 1 cup + 1 tablespoon all-purpose flour*

**FOR THE FILLING**

- 1 cup granulated sugar
- 3 tablespoons all-purpose flour
- 3 large eggs
- ½ cup lemon juice (from 2 lemons)

**FOR THE TOPPING**

- ½ cup powdered sugar
- Yellow gel or powdered food coloring

**Make a Color Poppin' Plate!** Serve with fresh raspberries.

Heat oven to 325°F. Line the bottom and sides of a 9×9-inch glass or ceramic baking pan with parchment paper, leaving an overhang on the sides.

**KIDS CAN HELP! For the crust:** In a medium bowl, combine the butter, sugar, vanilla, and salt; stir until thoroughly combined. Add the flour and stir until well mixed. Press firmly and evenly into the bottom of the pan, making sure to get in the corners.

Bake until the edges are lightly browned, about 20 minutes.

**KIDS CAN HELP! For the filling:** While the crust bakes, make the filling. In a large bowl, sift the sugar and flour together. Whisk in the eggs and lemon juice until completely combined.

Poke holes all over the top (but not all the way through) the partially baked crust. Pour the filling over the warm crust. Bake until the center is set and no longer jiggles, 22 to 25 minutes.

Remove from oven and let cool completely on a wire rack, about 2 hours. Chill in the refrigerator for an additional 1 to 2 hours. (Bars are best served chilled.)

**For the topping:** While bars are chilling, combine powdered sugar and a drop or two of the food coloring in a sealed container or zip-top plastic bag.

**KIDS CAN HELP!** Vigorously shake the sugar and food coloring to blend until it reaches the perfect shade of yummy yellow.

**To serve:** Very carefully lift the parchment handles out of the pan and place on a large cutting board. Dust uncut bars with the topping. Using a sharp knife, make six 1½-inch cuts on one side of the square. Make nine 1-inch cuts on an adjacent side of the square to make 54 little lemon bars. For neat and tidy squares, wipe the knife between each cut.

**\*Tip:** Sift flour, then measure.

# LASER LEMON-ADE

When the weather is hot and your crew needs some serious refreshment, nothing tastes better than freshly made lemonade. This is the real deal—just freshly squeezed lemon juice stirred together with a quick simple syrup to be as sweet or tart as you'd like.

ACTIVE TIME: 30 MINUTES
TOTAL TIME: 30 MINUTES +
COOLING TIME
MAKES ABOUT 10 SERVINGS

**FOR THE SIMPLE SYRUP**

1¾  cups sugar*

1  cup water

**FOR THE LEMONADE**

7  cups water, chilled

1½  cups fresh lemon juice and pulp
(from about 10 large lemons)**

Ice

Pink or yellow lemon
wheels, for garnish

**For the simple syrup:** In a small saucepan, combine the sugar and water. Bring to a boil, stirring to help sugar dissolve. When sugar is completely dissolved, set aside to cool. (Simple syrup can be made ahead and stored in the refrigerator.)

**KIDS CAN HELP! For the lemonade:** In a large pitcher, combine the chilled water and lemon juice and pulp. Stir in simple syrup to taste. Add ice and a few lemon wheels.

Serve in ice-filled glasses, garnished with a lemon wheel.

*Looking for sugar alternatives? Try maple syrup or agave nectar.

**Tip:** To get the most juice from your lemons, juice at room temperature (or even warm them in the microwave for 10 to 15 seconds). Roll on the counter a few times to loosen the pulp from the skin, then cut in half and juice. Add some—but not all—of the pulp to the juice when measuring. Be sure no seeds slip in.

**Make a Color Poppin' Plate!** Garnish edge of glass with a whole strawberry.

FOR AGES
**6+**

# MELTED CRAYON CONFETTI LANTERN

Make a colorful piece of home décor to create warm, flickering light on your dinner table. (Also a great way to repurpose crayons that are too small to draw with!)

## WHAT YOU NEED

Crayola Crayons of different colors, about 4

Crayon or pencil sharpener

Wax paper

Duct tape

Hair dryer

Scissors

Glass jar

Battery-operated fairy lights

## HOW YOU MAKE IT

Unwrap and sharpen your crayons into small shavings using the sharpener.

Tear off a square of wax paper and lay it on a flat protected surface. Sprinkle crayon shavings onto the wax paper. Be sure to blend the colors.

Place another piece of wax paper over top of your crayon shavings. Tape down the edges and squeeze out as many air bubbles as possible.

With adult assistance, use a hair dryer to melt the shavings until they form a colorful melted surface. Let cool.

Cut the wax paper to fit in a glass jar. Roll the wax paper and place inside the jar, wrapping around the inside edge of the glass.

Place battery-operated fairy lights in the jar to make a lantern.

# Totally Rad

# RED AND PINK

From rich scarlets to pastel pinks, red is radiant across the color spectrum. Sprinkle cereal with strawberries, sip on tomato soup, and stir red beans into your chili! Red foods are packed with vitamin A, which helps develop strong and healthy muscles, skin, and lungs. Let this dynamic color energize your body and mood.

# RAZZMATAZZ
# RASPBERRY SMOOTHIE

The addition of brilliantly hued raw beet brings eye-popping color to this sweet but healthful smoothie. It's loaded with nutrients such as potassium, magnesium, folate, and vitamin C.

ACTIVE: 5 MINUTES
TOTAL: 5 MINUTES
MAKES 2 SERVINGS

- 1½ cups apple juice, chilled
- 1 banana
- 1½ cups frozen raspberries
- 1 small raw red beet, peeled and diced
- ¾ cup vanilla Greek yogurt
- 1 tablespoon honey
- Fresh raspberries and mint leaves, for garnish (optional)

In a blender, combine the apple juice, banana, frozen raspberries, beet, yogurt, and honey. Blend until smooth.

**KIDS CAN HELP!** Divide between 2 glasses. Garnish with fresh raspberries and mint leaves, if desired.

**Make a Color Poppin' Plate!** Serve with **Glowing Green** Avocado Toast (page 86).

# RADICAL RED TOMATO SOUP WITH CHEESY CROUTONS

This creamy tomato soup is so much better than the canned stuff and takes only 30 minutes from start to finish, so you can make it for a quick lunch or busy weeknight supper. Here's a not-so-radical idea: Serve it with a grilled cheese sandwich for dipping!

ACTIVE TIME: 30 MINUTES
TOTAL TIME: 30 MINUTES
MAKES 4 SERVINGS

**FOR THE SOUP**

- ¼ cup (½ stick) butter
- 1 medium sweet onion, diced
- 4 tablespoons tomato paste
- 1 (28-ounce) can whole tomatoes
- 2 cups water
- ½ cup heavy whipping cream
- ½ teaspoon salt

**FOR THE CROUTONS**

- 2 tablespoons finely grated Parmesan cheese
- ¼ teaspoon sweet paprika
- 2 (6-inch) corn or flour tortillas
- 1 tablespoon butter, melted

**FOR SERVING**

- Whipping cream (optional)
- Cracked black pepper (optional)

**For the soup:** In a medium pot, melt the butter over medium heat. Add the onion and cook, stirring frequently, until translucent, 3 to 4 minutes. Add the tomato paste and cook, stirring constantly, until fragrant, about 1 minute.

Stir in the tomatoes and their juice and the water. Use a wooden spoon to break up the tomatoes. Bring to a boil, then reduce heat to low and simmer until liquid has reduced slightly, about 10 minutes.

Use an immersion blender to blend until very smooth. (Or blend in batches in a blender, then return all soup to pot). Stir in the whipping cream and reheat gently over low heat. Stir in the salt.

**For the croutons:** Heat oven to 350°F.

In a small bowl, stir together the cheese and paprika.

**KIDS CAN HELP!** Use mini cookie cutters (such as hearts, scallops, or stars) to cut shapes from the tortillas. Place on a parchment-lined baking pan. Brush with melted butter and sprinkle evenly with the cheese mixture. Bake until crisp, about 8 minutes.

**To serve:** Ladle the soup into bowls and top with the croutons. Drizzle with additional whipping cream and sprinkle with cracked black pepper, if desired.

**Make a Color Poppin' Plate!** Top each serving with bright green chopped fresh basil for contrasting colors and a bit of herby sweetness to balance out the acid of the tomato.

# CHERRY TOMATO & PEPPERONI PIZZA

Make family movie night extra-special with a homemade pizza that goes together in a snap with premade dough and sauce. The fresh mozzarella gives it a restaurant-quality touch.

ACTIVE TIME: 15 MINUTES
TOTAL TIME: 30 MINUTES
MAKES 6 SERVINGS

All-purpose flour

1 recipe Homemade Pizza Dough (recipe follows) or 1½ pounds purchased pizza dough

½ cup prepared pizza or marinara sauce

8 ounces fresh mozzarella cheese, thinly sliced

16 pepperoni slices

1 cup cherry or grape tomatoes, halved crosswise

6 fresh basil leaves, thinly sliced

Heat oven to 425°F.

Lightly flour a work surface. Roll the pizza dough out to desired thickness. Transfer to a parchment-lined baking sheet.

**KIDS CAN HELP!** Spread the sauce over the dough. Arrange the mozzarella slices over the sauce. Top with the pepperoni, then the tomatoes, cut side down.

Bake until crust is deep golden brown, cheese is melted, and pepperoni and tomatoes are very lightly charred, 15 to 20 minutes.

Top with basil leaves and serve.

**Homemade Pizza Dough:** In a large bowl, combine 1 cup warm water (120°F to 130°F) and 2¼ teaspoons active dry yeast (1 packet). Whisk to combine, and let stand 5 minutes or until foamy. Stir in 2½ cups flour, ⅓ cup olive oil, and ½ teaspoon salt. Beat with a wooden spoon until smooth, then stir in an additional ½ cup flour. Turn dough out onto a lightly floured work surface. Knead, adding up to ¼ cup additional flour a little bit at a time, to make a moderately stiff dough that is smooth and elastic (6 to 8 minutes). Shape into a ball and place in a lightly greased bowl, turning once to grease the dough's surface. Cover and let rise until double in size (about 1 hour). Punch dough down and let rest 5 minutes before using.

# PINKY PINK SHRIMP TACOS

How do you know your shrimp is properly cooked? It turns pink—maybe even Pinky Pink! Tacos made with street-taco-style tortillas are fun and perfectly sized for little hands.

ACTIVE TIME: 45 MINUTES
TOTAL TIME: 50 MINUTES
MAKES 4 SERVINGS (3 TACOS EACH)

### FOR THE LIME CREMA

- ½  cup sour cream or Greek yogurt
- 1  teaspoon lime zest
- 1  tablespoon lime juice
- ¼  teaspoon salt

### FOR THE PICO DE GALLO

- ½  small red onion, very finely chopped
- 4  small ripe tomatoes, seeded and very finely chopped
- 1  small jalapeño, seeded and very finely chopped (optional)
- ¼  cup finely chopped fresh cilantro
- 2  tablespoons fresh lime juice
- ¼  teaspoon salt, plus more to taste

### FOR THE SHRIMP

- 12  ounces small shrimp, tails removed
- 1  tablespoon + 2 teaspoons olive oil
- ¼  teaspoon salt
- ½  teaspoon chili powder

### FOR SERVING

- 12  street taco-size tortillas (corn or flour)
   Lime wedges

**KIDS CAN HELP! Make the lime crema:** In a small bowl, stir together the sour cream, lime zest, lime juice, and salt. Cover and refrigerate until ready to serve.

**For the pico de gallo:** In a medium bowl, stir together the onion, tomatoes, jalapeño, cilantro, lime juice, and the ¼ teaspoon salt. Taste and adjust seasonings if desired. Set aside until ready to serve.

**For the shrimp:** In a medium bowl, toss the shrimp with the 2 teaspoons olive oil, the salt, and chili powder. Heat a large nonstick skillet over medium-high heat. Add the 1 tablespoon oil to the pan. When shimmering, add the shrimp in a single layer. Cook shrimp until they are cooked through and turn pink with spots of red on the outside, 1 to 2 minutes per side.

**To serve:** Heat tortillas in a large skillet or on a griddle over medium-high heat until warmed and pliable, about 30 seconds per side. Divide shrimp among the tortillas. Drizzle with the lime crema and top with pico de gallo.

Serve with lime wedges.

**Make a Color Poppin' Plate!** Serve with packaged broccoli slaw tossed with bottled cilantro-lime dressing.

# **PIGGY PINK** PINWHEELS

These ham-and-cheese-stuffed puff pastry pinwheels make pretty party treats. Cherry preserves add a touch of sweetness, but you can substitute Dijon mustard if you'd like.

ACTIVE TIME: 20 MINUTES
TOTAL TIME: 35 MINUTES
MAKES 24 PINWHEELS

  All-purpose flour
1 sheet frozen puff pastry, thawed overnight in the refrigerator
1½ tablespoons cherry preserves
6 slices thinly sliced white Cheddar cheese
6 slices thinly sliced deli ham

Heat oven to 375°F. Line a rimmed baking sheet with parchment paper.

**KIDS CAN HELP!** Lightly flour a work surface. Lay puff pastry sheet on the surface and gently roll into a 10×12-inch rectangle. Spread with the cherry preserves, leaving a ½-inch border on all sides. Arrange the cheese slices on top, overlapping as needed. Top cheese with ham slices, overlapping as needed.

Starting at the long (12-inch) edge, roll the puff pastry into a log. Trim ends so they are even, then tightly wrap the log in plastic wrap. Chill until firm, about 30 minutes.

Using a sharp, serrated knife, carefully cut the log into 24 (½-inch) slices. Arrange the rolls on the prepared pan.

Bake until pastry is light golden brown and cheese is bubbly, 15 to 18 minutes.

Let cool 10 minutes before serving. Serve warm or at room temperature.

**Make a Color Poppin' Plate!** Add red and green apple slices to the serving platter.

# CUPCAKE SPRINKLES
## CUPCAKES

Red and pink sprinkles (sometimes called jimmies) in the batter make these vanilla cupcakes confetti cool! The buttercream frosting gets flavor and pretty-in-pink color from powdered freeze-dried raspberries.

ACTIVE TIME: 1 HOUR
TOTAL TIME: 1 HOUR
20 MINUTES + COOLING TIME
MAKES 12 CUPCAKES

### FOR THE CUPCAKES

- 1½ cups all-purpose flour
- 1½ teaspoons baking powder
- ¼ teaspoon salt
- ½ cup butter, softened
- ¾ cup sugar
- 3 large egg whites, at room temperature
- 1½ teaspoons clear vanilla extract
- ½ cup heavy whipping cream
- ½ cup red and pink sprinkles, plus more for decorating

### FOR THE RASPBERRY BUTTERCREAM

- ¾ cup freeze-dried raspberries
- 3½ cups powdered sugar
- 1 cup butter, at room temperature
- 1 teaspoon clear vanilla extract
- 3 tablespoons whole milk
- ⅛ teaspoon salt

**Make the cupcakes:** Line 12 standard muffin cups with paper liners.

Heat oven to 350°F. In a small bowl stir together the flour, baking powder, and salt. In a large mixing bowl, beat the butter with an electric mixer on medium-high for 30 seconds. Add the sugar, beating on medium-high for 1 minute. Scrape sides of bowl. Add the egg whites and vanilla extract; beat until combined.

Alternately add flour mixture and whipping cream to butter mixture, beating on low after each addition just until combined (batter will be thick). Using a spatula, stir in the sprinkles until evenly distributed.

**KIDS CAN HELP!** Spoon batter into prepared muffin cups, filling each about three-fourths full. Use the back of a spoon to smooth batter.

Bake until a wooden toothpick inserted in the centers comes out clean, about 20 minutes. Cool cupcakes in muffin cups on wire racks for 5 minutes. Remove cupcakes from muffin cups. Cool completely on wire racks. Frost with Raspberry Buttercream.

**Make the Raspberry Buttercream:** In a food processor or blender, grind the freeze-dried raspberries into a fine powder. Sift the powder with the powdered sugar, discarding any seeds.

In a large bowl, beat the butter on medium until fluffy and light in color, 5 to 10 minutes. Add the vanilla and milk, and mix on medium for 3 minutes.

Add the powdered sugar mixture 1 cup at a time, scraping the sides of the bowl after each addition. Add the salt and mix on low for an additional 30 seconds.

**KIDS CAN HELP!** To decorate the cupcakes, place frosting in a large pastry bag fitted with a large star or round tip. Pipe a swirl of frosting on each cupcake, ending with a peak and sprinkles on top.

# WILD WATERMELON
## JUICE FIZZY

What's the juiciest fruit? Watermelon, of course! Wring every drop out of the sweet stuff to make this refreshing summer sipper spiked with honey and lime juice and fizzed up with a splash of sparkling water.

ACTIVE TIME: 15 MINUTES
TOTAL TIME: 15 MINUTES
MAKES 6 SERVINGS

- 8 cups cubed seedless watermelon
- 2 tablespoons fresh lime juice
- 2 tablespoons honey
- Sparkling water, chilled
- Watermelon spears, for garnish

In a blender, blend the watermelon until completely smooth (do this in batches if necessary).

**KIDS CAN HELP!** Line a large bowl with cheesecloth. Pour the watermelon pulp into the bowl. Lift the cheesecloth out of the bowl, gathering the top of the cheesecloth, then squeezing to extract as much of the juice as possible.

**KIDS CAN HELP!** In large pitcher, combine watermelon juice, lime juice, and honey. Chill until serving time.

To serve, fill 6 glasses with ice. Fill glasses two thirds full with the watermelon juice mixture. Top off with sparkling water and garnish with the watermelon spears.

# TIE-DYE COFFEE FILTER FLOWERS CENTERPIECE

Make this bloomin' good bouquet, then decorate the dinner table with it!

**WHAT YOU NEED**

Coffee filters
Paper towels
Crayola Washable Markers
Crayola Paint Brush
Scissors
Chenille stems
Clean, dry jar
Decorative stones

**HOW TO MAKE IT**

Place a coffee filter on top of paper towels. Color with markers, then paint over with water. Repeat to make additional flowers. Let dry 1 to 2 hours.

**ADULT HELPER!** Using scissors, trim the colored paper towels to the same width as the colored coffee filters.

Place paper towel on top of filter. Fold in half twice. Twist bottom to make flower shape.

Wrap end of flower with a chenille stem.

Bunch the flowers together and wrap a chenille stem around flower stems to create a bouquet.

Fill the jar with decorative stones. Place bouquet in the jar to display.

# Outstanding ORANGE

Orange is so much more than a fruit! Audacious and unapologetic, this color begs to be noticed, and orange foods are no exception. Carrots, mangoes, peaches, sweet potatoes, cantaloupe, and butternut squash are packed with beta-carotene, which our bodies turn into vitamin A for immunity, antioxidants, and eye health. It may not give you X-ray vision, but see how much orange you can fit into your meals every week.

# BUTTERMILK-BROWN SUGAR **PEACH** PANCAKES

These fluffy griddle cakes are more than peachy! The sautéed fruit topping is flavored with maple syrup and cinnamon, and the cakes themselves with cinnamon and—if you like—crunchy pecans. Top it all off with whipped cream for a super-special breakfast or brunch.

ACTIVE TIME: 45 MINUTES
TOTAL TIME: 45 MINUTES
MAKES 4 SERVINGS

**FOR THE TOPPING**

- 2 tablespoons butter
- 1 tablespoon brown sugar
- ¼ teaspoon ground cinnamon
- 2 cups chopped peeled peaches (may be frozen, thawed)
- ½ cup pure maple syrup
- Whipped cream, for serving (optional)

**FOR THE PANCAKES**

- 1¾ cups all-purpose flour
- 2 tablespoons brown sugar
- 2 teaspoons baking powder
- ½ teaspoon baking soda
- ½ teaspoon ground cinnamon
- ¼ teaspoon salt
- 1 egg, lightly beaten
- 1½ cups buttermilk
- 3 tablespoons vegetable oil, plus more for frying
- ⅓ cup chopped pecans, plus more for garnish (optional)

**Make the topping:** In a medium nonstick skillet, melt the butter over medium heat. Stir in the brown sugar and cinnamon, and cook, stirring, until sugar is dissolved. Add the peaches and cook, stirring occasionally, until peaches just start to soften, 2 to 3 minutes. Add the maple syrup and cook, stirring occasionally, just until topping is heated through, 2 to 3 minutes. Cover and keep warm.

**KIDS CAN HELP! Make the pancakes:** In a large bowl, stir together the flour, brown sugar, baking powder, baking soda, cinnamon, and salt. In a small bowl, whisk together the egg, buttermilk, and the 3 tablespoons oil. Add egg mixture all at once to flour mixture. Stir just until moistened. Add the ⅓ cup pecans, if using.

To cook the pancakes, pour about ¼ cup batter on a hot, lightly greased griddle or heavy skillet over medium heat. (Spread batter if it is thick). Cook until pancakes are golden brown, turning when surfaces are bubbly and edges are slightly dry, 1 to 2 minutes per side.

Serve pancakes with peach topping. Top with whipped cream and additional pecans, if desired.

# MACARONI & CHEESE
## MAC & CHEESE

This quick and easy comfort food is on everyone's lists of favorites. It may take a bit more time than the boxed kind, but the cheese sauce is so easy you may never go back.

ACTIVE: 25 MINUTES
TOTAL: 35 MINUTES
MAKES 4 SERVINGS

- 8 ounces dried elbow macaroni (2 cups)
- 2 tablespoons butter
- 2 tablespoons all-purpose flour
- ⅛ teaspoon ground black pepper
- 1½ cups whole milk
- 3 cups shredded mild Cheddar with cream cheese

  Chopped cherry or grape tomatoes, for garnish (optional)

Cook macaroni according to package directions; drain.

Start the cheese sauce while the macaroni cooks. In a large saucepan, melt the butter over medium heat. Stir in the flour and pepper. Add the milk. Cook and stir until slightly thickened and bubbly. Add the cheese, stirring until melted. Stir cooked macaroni into cheese sauce in saucepan, stirring to coat. Cook over low heat for 2 to 3 minutes or until heated through, stirring frequently.

Let stand for 10 minutes before serving. Serve garnished with tomatoes, if desired.

**Make a Color Poppin' Plate!** For a colorful one-pot meal, stir in a cup or so of frozen peas or broccoli florets at the end of the pasta cooking time.

# GOLDEN NUGGET
## CHICKEN NUGGETS WITH HONEY-MUSTARD DIPPING SAUCE

Cheesy snack crackers make a crunchy coating for these chicken nuggets. Serve them with the sweet-savory honey mustard sauce, ranch dressing, or your favorite barbecue sauce.

ACTIVE TIME: 25 MINUTES
TOTAL TIME: 40 MINUTES
MAKES 4 TO 6 SERVINGS

**FOR THE CHICKEN**

Olive oil cooking spray

¼ cup sour cream, light sour cream, or low-fat Greek yogurt

1 large egg

½ teaspoon salt

½ teaspoon ground black pepper

½ teaspoon onion powder

½ teaspoon garlic powder

2 cups finely crushed cheese snack crackers

1½ pounds boneless, skinless chicken breasts, cut across the grain into 1-inch pieces

4 tablespoons butter, melted

**FOR THE DIPPING SAUCE**

¼ cup mayonnaise

¼ cup Dijon mustard

¼ cup honey

⅛ teaspoon paprika, smoked or sweet

**Make the chicken:** Heat oven to 375 °F. Spray a large rimmed baking pan with cooking spray.

**KIDS CAN HELP!** In a medium bowl, whisk together the sour cream, egg, salt, pepper, onion powder, and garlic powder. Add the chicken and toss well to coat.

**KIDS CAN HELP!** Pour the cracker crumbs onto a plate. Working with one piece at a time, coat the chicken in crumbs, pressing to help them adhere.

**KIDS CAN HELP!** Arrange in a single layer on the baking sheet, leaving as much room as possible between the pieces. Spray lightly with cooking spray, then gently drizzle the butter over the chicken.

Bake until breading is crisp and an instant-read thermometer inserted into the center of a nugget registers 165°F, about 15 minutes.

**KIDS CAN HELP! Make the dipping sauce:** While the chicken is baking, in a small bowl, whisk together the mayonnaise, mustard, honey, and paprika.

Let chicken stand for 5 minutes before serving with dipping sauce.

**Make a Color Poppin' Plate!** Try these with **Royal Purple** Cauliflower Bites (page 74) and Curly Noodles with **Pesto** (page 93).

# SASSY SALMON WITH GREEN ONION RICE

This flavorful teriyaki-style glazed salmon and rice combo is fancy enough for company but easy enough to make on a busy weeknight.

ACTIVE TIME: 45 MINUTES
TOTAL TIME: 45 MINUTES
MAKES 4 SERVINGS

## FOR THE SALMON

Vegetable oil

2 tablespoons teriyaki sauce

2 tablespoons hoisin sauce

2 tablespoons soy sauce

2 teaspoons toasted sesame oil

2 tablespoons brown sugar

1 large clove garlic, minced

1 teaspoon grated fresh ginger root

4 (5- to 6-ounce) salmon fillets

Sesame seeds, for garnish

## FOR THE RICE

1 tablespoon peanut or vegetable oil

4 green onions, thinly sliced (white and green parts kept separate)

1½ cups jasmine rice

1 (14.5-ounce) can chicken broth

1 cup water

½ teaspoon salt

¼ teaspoon ground black pepper

Heat oven to 400°F. Line a large rimmed baking pan with foil. Generously grease the foil with vegetable oil.

**KIDS CAN HELP! Make the salmon:** In a large bowl, whisk together the teriyaki sauce, hoisin sauce, soy sauce, sesame oil, brown sugar, garlic, and ginger. Add the salmon fillets to the bowl and toss gently to coat. Let marinate at room temperature for 20 minutes.

**Make the rice:** While the salmon marinates, heat the 1 tablespoon oil in a medium saucepan over medium heat. Add the scallion whites. Cook, stirring occasionally, until fragrant, 3 to 5 minutes.

Stir in the rice, broth, water, salt, and pepper. Bring to a boil; reduce to a simmer. Cover and cook until rice is tender and has absorbed the liquid, about 20 minutes. Remove from heat. Let stand, covered, 10 minutes more.

While rice is cooking, transfer salmon to the prepared pan. Bake until flaky and cooked through, 12 to 15 minutes.

Pour the marinade in a small saucepan and bring to a boil. Simmer, stirring occasionally, until thickened, 3 to 4 minutes.

**KIDS CAN HELP!** When salmon is out of the oven, brush with the teriyaki sauce and sprinkle with sesame seeds. After rice has stood for 10 minutes, stir green onion greens into rice and fluff with a fork.

Serve salmon with green onion rice.

**Make a Color Poppin' Plate!** Serve with sugar snap peas quick-sautéed in toasted sesame oil.

# NEON CARROT HUMMUS

Roasted carrots add a touch of sweetness and awesome orange color to this creamy dip. Swap the sweet paprika for smoked paprika for great smoky flavor.

ACTIVE TIME: 20 MINUTES
TOTAL TIME: 50 MINUTES
MAKES 3 CUPS

- 4 large carrots, peeled and cut into 2-inch chunks
- 2 tablespoons olive oil
- ½ teaspoon salt, plus more to taste
- ¼ teaspoon ground black pepper
- 1 (14.5-ounce) can chickpeas, drained and rinsed
- ¼ cup tahini (sesame paste)
- 1 teaspoon ground cumin
- 1 teaspoon sweet paprika
- 1 large clove garlic, roughly chopped
- 2 tablespoons lemon juice

  Pita chips and crunchy raw vegetables (such as sugar snap peas, radishes, baby sweet peppers, and/or broccoli and cauliflower florets), for serving

Heat oven to 400°F.

Place carrots in a large bowl and drizzle with the olive oil. Season with ½ teaspoon salt and the black pepper. Transfer to a large rimmed baking pan and roast until tender and just starting to brown, 30 to 35 minutes.

In a food processor or blender, combine the carrots, chickpeas, tahini, cumin, paprika, garlic, and lemon juice. Blend, drizzling in ⅓ to ½ cup water until smooth.

Taste and add salt, if desired.

Transfer to a serving dish and serve with pita chips and veggies.

**\*Note:** Kids can peel the carrots, then hand off the peeled carrots to an Adult Helper to cut.

**Make a Color Poppin' Plate!** Serve with a **Wild Watermelon** Juice Fizzy (page 45).

# OUTRAGEOUS ORANGE
## CREAMSICLE SHAKE

There's something outrageously delicious about the combination of vanilla and orange. This creamy, dreamy shake has ice cream-shop vibes but is super easy to make at home.

ACTIVE TIME: 10 MINUTES
TOTAL TIME: 10 MINUTES
MAKES 3 SERVINGS

- 1 cup firmly packed vanilla ice cream or frozen vanilla yogurt
- 1 cup firmly packed orange sherbet
- ½ teaspoon clear vanilla extract
- ⅔ cup whole milk
- Whipped cream and maraschino cherries, for garnish

In a blender, combine the ice cream, sherbet, vanilla extract, and milk. Blend until smooth.

**KIDS CAN HELP!** Divide mixture among 3 glasses. Top each serving with whipped cream and a cherry.

Serve immediately.

# MANGO TANGO LASSI

Lassi is a refreshing mango-and-yogurt drink that's popular in India. You'll do a happy dance with every sip! This is a nice beverage to accompany **Unmellow Yellow** Pineapple-Fried Rice (page 21) or **Spring Green** Two-Pea Stir Fry with Tofu (page 90).

ACTIVE TIME: 10 MINUTES
TOTAL TIME: 10 MINUTES
MAKES 2 SERVINGS

1½  cups cubed mango (use very ripe fresh or frozen, thawed)

1  cup plain low-fat yogurt (not Greek)

½  cup cold milk

4  teaspoons honey

Pinch of cardamom (optional)

1  teaspoon finely chopped roasted pistachios, for garnish (optional)

In a blender, combine the mango, yogurt, milk, honey, and cardamom, if using. Blend until smooth, adding a little water or a few ice cubes to adjust to desired consistency.

**KIDS CAN HELP!** Divide mixture between 2 tall glasses. Sprinkle with chopped pistachios, if desired.

# FAMILY MOVIE NIGHT SNACK HOLDER

Make movie night at home extra-special with a DIY tray for holding popcorn, drinks, and candies.

## WHAT YOU NEED

Lightweight cups

Paper bag

Pencil

Upcycled box

Scissors

Crayola Paint Brush

Crayola Washable Paint

Crayola Bright Pop! Cardstock

Crayola No-Run School Glue

Crayola Crayons

Construction Paper

Crayola Take Note
Permanent Markers

Crayola Glitter Glue

## HOW TO MAKE IT

**To create Movie Night Tray:** Using a cup and the paper bag as a guide, trace drink and snack openings on top of the box.

**ADULT HELPER!** Use scissors to cut out openings.

Paint box with two layers of paint, allowing to dry 1 to 2 hours between coats. Cut cardstock to fit sides of box. Glue cardstock and write name with permanent markers on sides of box.

**To create DIY Popcorn Bag:** Sketch and cut scalloped pattern on top of bag. Color red stripes with crayons.

Use construction paper, cardstock, and permanent markers to create the "popcorn" label and glue to bag. Embellish with construction paper, permanent markers, and glitter glue. Dry 3 to 4 hours.

Fill DIY Popcorn Bag with popcorn. Add drink and sweet snack of choice to Movie Night Tray cup holders to enjoy while watching your favorite flick!

# *Bold*
# BLUE
## *and*
# PURPLE

From the skies to the seas, calming, classic blue is always reliable and pairs well with its elegant cousin purple. Incorporate these cool colors into your day with blueberries on oatmeal, blue corn chips with salsa, purple cabbage in stir-fry, and bunches of purple grapes for a snack. Blue and purple foods are high in antioxidants, which can help prevent some serious diseases—and they boost your brain to boot!

# BLUE BERRY BLUE MUFFINS

Bake up a batch of these tender, blueberry-studded muffins for a special breakfast or brunch or as an afternoon pick-me-up with a glass of cold milk or hot tea. Freeze-dried blueberry powder gives the icing fruity flavor and a super-cool hue.

ACTIVE TIME: 20 MINUTES
TOTAL TIME: 40 MINUTES +
COOLING TIME
MAKES 12 MUFFINS

**FOR THE MUFFINS**

  Nonstick baking spray
2 cups all-purpose flour
¾ cup sugar
2½ teaspoons baking powder
½ teaspoon salt
2 eggs, beaten
¾ cup milk
½ cup butter, melted
2 teaspoons lemon zest
1 cup fresh or frozen blueberries, thawed

**FOR THE ICING**

1¼ cups powdered sugar
2 to 3 tablespoons milk
4 tablespoons freeze-dried blueberry powder

**Make the muffins:** Heat oven to 375°F.

Spray 12 standard muffins cups with baking spray. Set aside.

**KIDS CAN HELP!** In a medium bowl, stir together the flour, sugar, baking powder, and salt. Make a well in the center of dry mixture; set aside.

**KIDS CAN HELP!** In a medium bowl, whisk together the eggs, milk, butter, and lemon zest; add all at once to the dry mixture. Stir just until moistened (batter should be lumpy). Fold in blueberries. Spoon batter into prepared muffin cups, filling each almost full.

Bake until golden, about 20 minutes. Cool in muffin cups on a wire rack for 5 minutes. Remove muffins from pan and allow to cool for 15 to 20 minutes before icing.

**Make the icing:** In a medium bowl, whisk together the powdered sugar and 2 tablespoons of the milk. Whisk in the powdered blueberries. Add more milk, if necessary, to achieve desired consistency.

**KIDS CAN HELP!** Place a piece of waxed paper under the cooling rack with the muffins on it. Drizzle the icing over the muffins. Allow to set for 15 to 20 minutes before serving.

**Make a Color Poppin' Plate!** Serve with easy-to-peel clementines or mandarin oranges.

# BLUE BLAZES NACHOS

These cheesy, crispy nachos are loaded with 10-minute homemade refried black beans and a whole host of other goodies. Quick enough for lunch, special enough for a party! If you'd like, swap the avocado for a few dollops of **Twist o' Lime** Guacamole (page 94).

ACTIVE TIME: 30 MINUTES
TOTAL TIME: 40 MINUTES
MAKES 4 SERVINGS

### FOR THE BEANS

- 2 tablespoons olive oil
- ¼ teaspoon garlic powder
- ¼ teaspoon onion powder
- ½ teaspoon ground cumin
- 1 (15-ounce) can black beans
- ¼ teaspoon salt
- ¼ teaspoon ground black pepper

### FOR THE NACHOS

- Olive oil cooking spray
- 4 cups blue corn tortilla chips
- ½ cup sliced green onions
- 2 cups shredded Mexican cheese blend
- ¾ cup diced avocado
- Fresh cilantro leaves
- Sour cream and salsa verde, for serving

Heat oven to 400°F.

**Make the beans:** Place a colander over a bowl. Drain the beans, reserving the liquid.

In a medium nonstick skillet, heat the olive oil over medium heat. Add the garlic powder, onion powder, and cumin. Cook, stirring constantly, until fragrant, about 1 minute.

Add the beans to the skillet. Cook, stirring frequently, until heated through, 5 to 6 minutes.

Use a potato masher to mash the beans until creamy but still textured. Add small amounts of the bean liquid, mashing and stirring, until you achieve the desired consistency.

Season with salt and pepper. Set aside.

**KIDS CAN HELP! Make the nachos:** Line a large rimmed baking pan with foil. Spray the foil with olive oil cooking spray. Spread half of the chips evenly on the pan. Spoon about half of the black bean mixture over the chips. Top with half of the green onions and cheese. Repeat layers, ending with cheese.

Bake until cheese is melted, 10 to 12 minutes.

Top with avocado and cilantro leaves. Serve immediately with sour cream and salsa.

**Make a Color Poppin' Plate!** Top the nachos with quartered red, yellow, and orange cherry tomatoes along with the avocado.

# MAUVELOUS
## CABBAGE STIR-FRY

Yes, that rice is purple—and it's all natural. Also called black rice, emperor's rice, or forbidden rice, purple rice is widely available in supermarkets and online. In addition to being beautifully colored, it is far more nutritious than white rice.

ACTIVE TIME: 40 MINUTES
TOTAL TIME: 40 MINUTES
MAKES 4 SERVINGS

- 2 cloves garlic, minced
- 1 tablespoon grated fresh ginger root
- ¼ to ½ teaspoon crushed red pepper (optional)
- ½ teaspoon five-spice powder
- ¼ cup low-sodium soy sauce
- 2 tablespoons rice vinegar
- 1 teaspoon toasted sesame oil
- 1 tablespoon pure maple syrup
- 2 tablespoons peanut or vegetable oil
- ¾ pound ground chicken or turkey
- 1 small purple cabbage (about 1 pound), cored and thinly sliced (about 6 cups)
- 6 green onions, very thinly sliced
- ½ cup chopped fresh cilantro
  Hot cooked purple rice, for serving
  Black and white sesame seeds, for garnish (optional)

**KIDS CAN HELP!** In a small bowl, combine the garlic, ginger, red pepper (if using), and five-spice powder. In a second small bowl, combine 2 tablespoons of the soy sauce, the vinegar, sesame oil, and maple syrup.

In a large, deep skillet or wok with a lid, heat 1 tablespoon of the peanut oil over medium-high heat. When hot, add the chicken and garlic-ginger mixture. Cook, breaking up the meat with a wooden spoon. Add the remaining 2 tablespoons soy sauce. Cook, stirring frequently, until meat is cooked through and any liquid that has accumulated has mostly evaporated, about 5 minutes. Transfer to a bowl.

Add the remaining 1 tablespoon peanut oil to the skillet. Add the cabbage. Cook, stirring occasionally, until cabbage just starts to wilt. Add the soy sauce-vinegar mixture. Cover the skillet and cook over high heat for 1 minute, until cabbage is wilted but not mushy.

Uncover and stir in the green onions, cilantro, and reserved chicken and any juices. Cook and stir for an additional 30 seconds. The cabbage should be crisp-tender. (If it's not, cook a little longer.)

Serve over hot cooked purple rice. Garnish with sesame seeds, if desired.

**Make a Color Poppin' Plate!** Garnish with additional fresh cilantro leaves.

# ROYAL PURPLE
# CAULIFLOWER BITES

The color in this vibrantly hued king of cauliflower comes from the same antioxidant found in red cabbage, called anthocyanin. The more sun the cabbage heads get as they grow, the deeper the color. Purple cauliflower doesn't taste any different than white cauliflower—it just looks a lot different! Like white cauliflower, it gets crispy and delicious when roasted with oil, butter, or ghee and seasonings.

**ACTIVE TIME: 15 MINUTES**
**TOTAL TIME: 50 MINUTES**
**MAKES 4 SERVINGS**

- 4 tablespoons ghee, melted
- ½ teaspoon ground cumin
- 1 teaspoon garam masala
- ½ teaspoon salt
- 1 head purple cauliflower, cut into 2-inch florets
  Chopped fresh chives, for garnish (optional)

Heat oven to 425°F. Line a large rimmed baking pan with foil.

In a large bowl, whisk together the ghee, cumin, garam masala, and salt until well blended.

**KIDS CAN HELP!** Add cauliflower florets and toss to combine. Arrange florets on the prepared pan in a single layer.

Roast until stems are tender and florets are crisp and golden brown on the edges, 35 to 40 minutes.

Garnish with fresh chives, if desired.

# POPPIN' PURPLE
## POTATO CHIPS WITH FRENCH ONION DIP

Up your chips-and-dip game with crispy oven-fried purple potato chips and a quick and creamy homemade French onion dip. If you can't find purple potatoes (also called blue potatoes), regular russet potatoes work, too. They'll still be poppin'—just not purple!

ACTIVE TIME: 30 MINUTES
TOTAL TIME: 1 HOUR 30 MINUTES
MAKES 4 SERVINGS

### FOR THE DIP

- 1 cup sour cream or Greek yogurt
- 1 tablespoon dried minced onion
- 1 teaspoon onion powder
- 1/8 teaspoon garlic powder
- 1/4 teaspoon salt
- 1/8 teaspoon ground black pepper
- 1 tablespoon finely chopped fresh parsley

### FOR THE POTATO CHIPS

- 1 pound purple potatoes, scrubbed and dried
- 2 tablespoons olive oil
- 1 teaspoon salt

**KIDS CAN HELP! Make the dip:** In a small bowl, stir together the sour cream, dried onion, onion powder, garlic powder, salt, pepper, and parsley.

Refrigerate for 1 hour to allow the flavors to meld and the dried onion to soften.

**Make the potato chips:** Heat oven to 400°F. Line two large rimmed baking pans with parchment paper. Use a mandoline to slice the potatoes 1/16 inch thick. (If you don't have a mandoline, use a sharp knife to slice them as thinly as you possibly can.) Pat both sides of the sliced potatoes dry with paper towels.

Place the potatoes in a large bowl and toss with the olive oil and salt. Arrange the potato slices in a single layer on the baking sheets, being careful to avoid overlap. Bake for 10 minutes. Remove pans from the oven and turn each chip. Bake an additional 7 to 9 minutes, carefully watching to avoid burning. Remove any chips that seem done to a wire rack.

Let cool for 10 to 12 minutes until crisp (chips will continue to crisp as they cool).

Serve chips with dip.

**Make a Color Poppin' Plate!** Serve with
Laser Lemon-ade (page 26).

# BLUETIFUL
## MIXED-BERRY CRISP

A generous layer of rich and buttery oat crumble tops the warm berry trio of blueberries, blackberries, and raspberries. Serve it warm with a scoop of vanilla ice cream.

ACTIVE TIME: 15 MINUTES
TOTAL TIME: 50 MINUTES +
COOLING TIME
MAKES 8 SERVINGS

- 1½ cups blueberries (fresh or frozen, thawed)
- 1½ cups blackberries (fresh or frozen, thawed)
- 1 cup raspberries (fresh or frozen, thawed)
- ¾ cup all-purpose flour
- 2 tablespoons granulated sugar
- 1 cup old-fashioned rolled oats
- 1 cup packed brown sugar
- ½ teaspoon ground cinnamon
- ½ cup cold butter, cut into large chunks
- Vanilla ice cream or frozen vanilla yogurt, for serving

Heat oven to 350°F.

**KIDS CAN HELP!** Place the blueberries, blackberries, and raspberries in an 8×8-inch square glass baking dish. Sprinkle with ¼ cup of the flour and the granulated sugar; gently toss until all berries are coated.

**KIDS CAN HELP!** In a medium bowl, mix together the oats, brown sugar, remaining ½ cup flour, and cinnamon. Cut butter into oat mixture with a fork or pastry blender until mixture is crumbly. Spoon over berry mixture.

Bake until crisp is golden brown, 35 to 40 minutes. Let stand 15 to 20 minutes before serving warm with ice cream.

# B'DAZZLED BLUE
## BUTTERFLY PEA
## FLOWER TEA LATTE

Butterfly pea flowers are dried and used to make tea in parts of South America and Asia—particularly Thailand. They can be turned into powder or extract, too. Whatever they're used in turns a magical shade of blue, including this warming honey-sweetened latte.

ACTIVE TIME: 10 MINUTES
TOTAL TIME: 10 MINUTES
MAKES 1 SERVING

- 1 teaspoon butterfly pea flower powder
- 1 tablespoon very hot water
- 1 to 2 teaspoons honey
  Few drops vanilla extract
- 1 cup milk, heated

In a 10- to 12-ounce mug, combine the butterfly pea flower powder and hot water. Whisk until smooth. Add the honey and vanilla.

**KIDS CAN HELP!** Pour milk into a small jar with a lid. Cover tightly and shake until frothy. Pour into the mug. Serve immediately.

**Make a Color Poppin' Plate!** Serve with orange sections or slices.

# PLACE CARD HOLDERS

Create place card holders for a special family dinner or holiday—or just because!

## WHAT YOU NEED

Cookie cutters of choice (optional)

Crayola Model Magic®

Scissors

Chenille stems

Construction paper

Crayola Signature Sketch & Detail Dual Ended Markers

Crayola Signature Gel Pens

## HOW YOU MAKE IT

For each place card holder, shape or use cookie cutters to cut the Model Magic into a design of choice.

Cut the chenille stems to fit and insert into the top of the place card holder. Dry overnight.

**ADULT HELPER!** For each place card, cut a small rectangular piece of construction paper. Use markers to write name and gel pens to add flourishes.

Bend or twist the top of the chenille stem slightly to hold place card. Place the card in the chenille stem.

Set place card holders on table.

# Great GREENS

Earthly, vigorous green is a sign of growth, vitality, and the transition to spring after a long winter. The great thing about green foods is that they can be easily found fresh in grocery stores and farmers markets year-round. Broccoli and Brussels sprouts (try them roasted—it reduces the bitterness) are high in calcium, and leafy greens like spinach and kale are full of fiber and vitamins. Green isn't just easy, it's essential.

# GLOWING GREEN
## AVOCADO TOAST

Enjoy this creamy avocado spread on a piece of whole-grain toast for breakfast and you'll be glowing all day!

**ACTIVE TIME: 15 MINUTES**
**TOTAL TIME: 15 MINUTES**
**MAKES 2 SERVINGS**

1 medium ripe avocado, halved and pitted

2 teaspoons fresh lemon juice

¼ teaspoon salt

1 green onion, trimmed and thinly sliced

2 thick slices whole-grain bread, toasted

1 teaspoon everything bagel seasoning

**KIDS CAN HELP!** Scoop the avocado flesh into a bowl. Add the lemon juice and salt. Using a fork or a potato masher, mash the avocado to desired consistency. Stir in the green onion.

**KIDS CAN HELP!** Spread the avocado mixture on the toast. Sprinkle with everything bagel seasoning. Serve immediately.

**Make a Color Poppin' Plate!** Serve with purple grapes.

# SHEEN GREEN
## BROCCOLI-CHEESE SOUP

Creamy, cheesy, and packed with nutrients—including fiber, vitamins C and K, iron, and potassium—this comforting soup is like a big, warm hug served up with a spoon. Try it with crunchy saltines on the side.

ACTIVE TIME: 30 MINUTES
TOTAL TIME: 30 MINUTES
MAKES 4 SERVINGS

  4   cups fresh broccoli florets
1½   cups chicken broth, divided
  1   tablespoon butter
  1   tablespoon all-purpose flour
  ½   teaspoon lemon zest
  ½   teaspoon salt, plus
        more to taste
  ¼   teaspoon ground black
        pepper, plus more to taste
  1   cup whole milk or half-and-
        half, plus more as needed
  1   cup shredded mild Cheddar
        cheese, plus more for garnish*

**KIDS CAN HELP!** Place the broccoli florets and 2 tablespoons water in a covered microwave-safe dish. Cook on high for 3 to 4 minutes or until crisp-tender and bright green, stirring once. Drain and set aside 1 cup of the florets.

In a food processor or blender, combine the remaining 3 cups florets and ¾ cup of the chicken broth. Cover and process or blend until smooth; set aside.

In a medium saucepan, melt the butter over medium heat. Whisk in the flour, lemon zest, ½ teaspoon salt, and ¼ teaspoon pepper. Add 1 cup milk. Cook and stir until slightly thickened and bubbly. Cook and stir for 1 minute more.

Stir in the reserved 1 cup florets, the blended broccoli mixture, remaining ¾ cup broth, and the 1 cup cheese. Cook and stir until heated through. If necessary, stir in additional milk to reach desired consistency. Season to taste with additional salt and pepper.

**\*Note:** Kids can shred a block of cheese on a box grater and measure out 1 cup.

**Make a Color Poppin' Plate!** Serve with wedges of warm corn bread.

# SPRING GREEN TWO-PEA STIR-FRY WITH TOFU

When winter is over and things are starting to green up, celebrate with this vibrant, healthy stir-fry. Those who think they don't like tofu may find themselves captivated by the golden-brown crisp-on-the-outside, creamy-on-the-inside cubes.

ACTIVE TIME: 35 MINUTES
TOTAL TIME: 35 MINUTES
MAKES 4 SERVINGS

¼ cup soy sauce

2 tablespoons mirin or orange juice

1 tablespoon granulated sugar

2 teaspoons cornstarch

1 teaspoon rice vinegar

2 tablespoons peanut oil or vegetable oil

1 (12- to 14-ounce) package firm tofu, patted dry and cut into large dice

8 ounces shiitake mushrooms, stems removed, caps sliced

4 medium cloves garlic, thinly sliced

2 teaspoons grated fresh ginger root

8 ounces snow peas

8 ounces sugar snap peas

1 tablespoon sesame seeds

Hot cooked rice, for serving

**KIDS CAN HELP!** In a small bowl, whisk together the soy sauce, mirin, sugar, cornstarch, and vinegar; set aside.

In a large nonstick skillet, heat 1 tablespoon of the oil over high heat. When it smokes, add the tofu and cook until golden brown on all sides, about 3 minutes. Remove to a plate and set aside.

Reduce heat to medium. Add the remaining 1 tablespoon oil. Add the mushrooms and cook, stirring frequently, until tender and starting to brown, 4 to 5 minutes. Add the garlic and ginger, and cook until garlic starts to brown, about 1 minute. Add the snow peas, sugar snap peas, and sesame seeds, and cook, stirring frequently, until peas are bright green, slightly softened, yet still crisp, about 5 minutes.

Add reserved tofu and soy sauce mixture, and cook just until tofu is warm and sauce has thickened slightly, about 1 minute more.

Serve over hot cooked rice.

# CURLY NOODLES
# WITH **PESTO**

The spirals in the rotini pasta are perfect for capturing the yummy pesto sauce. To store any leftover pesto, cover the surface with plastic wrap (to keep it from turning brown) and refrigerate for up to 1 week. It can also be frozen in a tightly sealed container for up to 3 months.

ACTIVE TIME: 20 MINUTES
TOTAL TIME: 35 MINUTES
MAKES 4 SERVINGS

12   ounces dried rotini (corkscrew) pasta
⅓   cup + 2 tablespoons olive oil
2   cups firmly packed fresh basil leaves, plus chopped basil for garnish*
½   cup pine nuts, toasted
2   cloves garlic, peeled and coarsely chopped
¼   teaspoon salt
¾   cup grated Parmesan cheese

Cook the pasta according to package directions. While the pasta is cooking, make the pesto.

In a food processor bowl, combine the ⅓ cup olive oil, the 2 cups basil, the pine nuts, garlic, and salt. Cover and process until nearly smooth, stopping and scraping sides as necessary. Stir in Parmesan.

Add enough of the additional 2 tablespoons olive oil to reach desired consistency.

When pasta is done cooking to al dente, remove about 1 cup of the pasta cooking water from the pot, then drain the pasta. Return the pasta to the pot, then add desired amount of pesto. Stir to combine, adding more pesto if desired.

To make the sauce creamier, add a little bit of the pasta water, a tablespoon at a time, until you reach the desired consistency.

Divide among four shallow bowls. Garnish with chopped basil and serve immediately.

***Note:** Kids can measure out the basil leaves.

**Make a Color Poppin' Plate!** Top each serving with halved or quartered red, yellow, and/or orange cherry tomatoes.

# TWIST O' LIME GUACAMOLE

What is served at almost every party—and usually the most popular dish? Creamy, lime-spiked avocado dip served with crunchy tortilla chips. This version has a generous dose of fresh lime juice, of course—and if you'd like, you can even add more.

ACTIVE TIME: 20 MINUTES
TOTAL TIME: 20 MINUTES
MAKES 6 SERVINGS

- 2 ripe avocados, halved and pitted
- ¼ teaspoon salt, plus more to taste
- 2 tablespoons fresh lime juice
- 2 tablespoons minced red onion
- 1 jalapeño chile, seeded and minced (optional)
- ¼ cup fresh cilantro leaves, chopped
- ⅛ teaspoon ground black pepper
- 1 roma tomato, seeded and chopped (optional)

Tortilla chips, for serving

**KIDS CAN HELP!** Scoop the avocado flesh into a medium bowl. Using a fork or potato masher, roughly mash the avocados.

Add the ¼ teaspoon salt, the lime juice, red onion, jalapeño (if using), cilantro, black pepper, and tomato (if using). Stir to combine. Taste and add more salt and black pepper, if desired.

Serve with tortilla chips.

**\*Tip:** If you're making the guacamole a couple of hours ahead of serving time, cover the surface with plastic wrap and refrigerate. Let it come to room temperature before serving.

**Make a Color Poppin' Plate!** Top with halved cherry or grape tomatoes or matchstick-cut radishes.

# **KIWI**-KEY LIME TARTLETS

What's better than a piece of pie? Your very own pie! These individual graham cracker-crust tartlets are filled with a creamy lime filling and topped with sweet-tart kiwi—a perfect make-ahead summer dessert.

ACTIVE TIME: 20 MINUTES
TOTAL TIME: 20 MINUTES +
2 HOURS CHILLING TIME
MAKES 8 SERVINGS

- 1 (8-ounce) package cream cheese or light cream cheese (neufchâtel), softened
- ⅔ cup sugar
- 3 tablespoons fresh key lime juice
- 2 tablespoons key lime zest
- 1 (8-ounce) container frozen nondairy whipped topping, thawed
- 2 (6-count) package graham cracker tartlet crusts
- 2 kiwifruits

In a large bowl, combine the cream cheese, sugar, juice, and zest with an electric mixer on medium-high. Add the whipped topping and incorporate into the cream cheese mixture on low.

**KIDS CAN HELP!** Divide the filling among 8 tartlet crusts (save the remaining 4 for another recipe). Refrigerate for 2 hours to firm up.

Right before serving, peel and slice the kiwifruits. Cut the slices in half. Garnish the tartlets with the halved slices of kiwi.

# CARIBBEAN SEA COOLER

This creamy green sipper makes for smooth sailing when you're in need of a boost any time of day.

ACTIVE TIME: 5 MINUTES
TOTAL TIME: 5 MINUTES
MAKES 2 SERVINGS

1 cup frozen pineapple chunks
2 cups baby spinach leaves
1 cup apple juice
1 cup coconut milk
1 tablespoon lime juice
  Fresh pineapple wedges and
  lime wheels, for garnish

In a blender, combine the pineapple, spinach, apple juice, coconut milk, and lime juice. Blend until smooth.

**KIDS CAN HELP!** Divide mixure between 2 glasses. Garnish with pineapple wedges and lime wheels.

# DONUT COASTERS

Coast to a cool-looking table with these DIY donut coasters!

## WHAT YOU NEED

Crayola Acrylic Paint

Disposable cup

Craft Stick

Crayola Paint Brush

Round cork coasters

Crayola Glitter Glue

## HOW YOU MAKE IT

Mix the paint color of your choice in a disposable cup.

Paint donut frosting on a coaster, leaving the center unpainted. Dry 1 to 2 hours. Add a second coat. Dry 1 to 2 hours.

Repeat steps 1 and 2 to create a set of coasters.

Add donut designs and details with glitter glue. Dry 3 to 4 hours.

Use coasters under your drink of choice.

# Beautiful BROWN

Humble brown may not be the brightest color in the box, but as far as food goes, it has lots going for it: warm buttered toast, nourishing bran muffins, creamy whole-wheat spaghetti with mushrooms, and—perhaps most famously—chocolate. Starting with a basic brown is a blank canvas to build something sweet, savory, or a bit of both.

# MINI BROWN BRAN MUFFINS

These hearty little muffins are small but mighty! They're loaded with fiber from whole-bran cereal and made tasty with brown sugar, maple syrup, and a smattering of sweet currants in every bite.

ACTIVE TIME: 20 MINUTES
TOTAL TIME: 35 MINUTES
MAKES 36 MINI MUFFINS

- 2⅔ cups whole-bran cereal (such as All-Bran®)
- 1⅔ cups buttermilk
- ½ cup whole wheat flour
- ½ cup all-purpose flour
- 1¾ teaspoons baking powder
- ¼ teaspoon baking soda
- ¼ cup vegetable oil, plus more for greasing the pan
- 2 tablespoons butter, softened
- ⅓ cup packed brown sugar
- 2 large eggs
- ¼ cup pure maple syrup
- ½ cup currants

Heat oven to 350°F. Lightly grease 36 mini muffin cups with vegetable oil; set aside.

**KIDS CAN HELP!** Place the bran cereal in a medium bowl. Pour the buttermilk over the cereal. Let stand 5 to 10 minutes or until cereal is softened.

**KIDS CAN HELP!** In a small bowl, stir together the flour, baking powder, and baking soda.

In a large bowl, beat the oil and butter with an electric mixer on medium for 30 seconds. Add the brown sugar. Beat until fluffy, about 30 seconds. Beat in the eggs, one at a time, until mixed. Add the maple syrup; beat until combined. Add cereal mixture and flour mixture to egg mixture, stirring just until combined. Stir in the currants. Spoon batter into prepared muffin cups, mounding it slightly.

Bake until tops are golden and centers are firm to the touch, about 20 to 25 minutes.

Cool in muffin cups on a wire rack for 5 minutes. Remove from pan to rack. Serve warm.

**Make a Color Poppin' Plate!** Serve with fresh strawberries and/or orange slices.

# TINY TOAD BROWN SAUSAGE PUFFS

These little sausage puffs are a play on the classic English dish of toad-in-the-hole: full-size sausages baked in a casserole in Yorkshire pudding batter (similar to popovers) and served with gravy. Kids can portion out the sausages in each muffin cup.

ACTIVE TIME: 30 MINUTES
TOTAL TIME: 1 HOUR
MAKES 6 SERVINGS (2 PUFFS EACH)

### FOR THE PUFFS
- 24  cocktail sausages
- 2  tablespoons vegetable oil
- 1  cup + 2 tablespoons all-purpose flour
- ½  teaspoon dry mustard (optional)
- 3  large eggs
- 1  cup + 2 tablespoons whole milk
- ¼  teaspoon salt
- ¼  teaspoon ground black pepper
- 1  tablespoon thinly sliced fresh chives

### FOR THE GRAVY
- 1  tablespoon butter
- ¼  cup finely chopped red onion
-    Pinch of sugar
- 1  (0.87-ounce) package brown gravy mix
-    Worcestershire sauce

### FOR SERVING
-    Mashed potatoes and steamed buttered green peas

**Make the puffs:** Heat oven to 425°F.

**KIDS CAN HELP!** Place 2 sausages in each of 12 standard-size muffin cups. Drizzle the sausages with the oil. Bake until sausages have browned, about 5 to 10 minutes.

**KIDS CAN HELP!** While sausages are browning, combine the flour and dry mustard (if using) in a medium bowl. Whisk to combine. Crack the eggs into a 4-cup measuring cup and whisk until smooth. Add the milk and whisk again to combine.

**KIDS CAN HELP!** Make a well in the center of the flour mixture and pour in the egg mixture. Whisk to combine. Add the salt, pepper, and chives, and stir to combine. Pour the batter into the 4-cup measuring cup.

Remove the muffin tin from the oven and place on a heatproof surface. Very carefully divide the batter among the muffin cups.

Return to the oven and bake until puffed and golden brown, about 15 minutes.

**Make the gravy:** While the puffs are baking, melt the butter in a small saucepan over medium-low. Add the onion and a pinch of sugar. Cook, stirring frequently, until softened and starting to brown, 5 to 10 minutes.

Add 1 cup cold water and the gravy mix, whisking to combine. Bring to a boil over medium, stirring frequently, then reduce heat to low and simmer until thickened slightly, about 1 minute. Season with a dash or two of Worcestershire sauce.

**To serve:** Let puffs stand for 4 to 5 minutes to cool slightly. Serve with gravy, mashed potatoes, and peas.

# TUMBLEWEED SPAGHETTI WITH CREAMY MUSHROOM-BACON SAUCE

You'll be blown away by the deliciousness of this creamy bacon-studded pasta dish! If you'd like, add ¼ cup snipped rehydrated dried or oil-packed sun-dried tomatoes along with the chopped parsley.

**ACTIVE TIME: 30 MINUTES**
**TOTAL TIME: 30 MINUTES**
**MAKES 6 SERVINGS**

- 4 slices thick-cut bacon, chopped
- 16 ounces cremini mushrooms, stem ends trimmed, sliced
- 2 cloves garlic, minced
- ¼ teaspoon salt
- ¼ teaspoon ground black pepper
- 12 ounces whole-wheat spaghetti
- ½ cup heavy whipping cream
- ½ cup chicken broth
- 1 tablespoon balsamic vinegar
- ¼ cup chopped fresh curly-leaf parsley, plus more for garnish
  Grated Parmesan cheese, for garnish

In a large nonstick skillet, cook the bacon over medium until browned and crisp. Transfer to a paper towel-lined plate to drain, reserving drippings.

Add the mushrooms, garlic, salt, and pepper to skillet. Cook, stirring frequently, until mushrooms are tender and browned, 8 to 10 minutes.

Meanwhile, cook the pasta according to package directions; drain, reserving about 1 cup pasta cooking water.

Add the cream and broth to mushrooms. Cook until bubbly and slightly thickened, 1 to 2 minutes. Add bacon to skillet. Stir in pasta, vinegar, and the ¼ cup parsley; heat through. (If sauce is too thick, add a little reserved pasta cooking water to loosen.)

**KIDS CAN HELP!** Divide pasta mixture among 6 shallow bowls. Swirl pasta into three "tumbleweeds." Garnish with chopped parsley and cheese.

**Make a Color Poppin' Plate!** Serve with a Bibb lettuce salad topped with grape tomatoes and sliced mini cucumbers.

# COPPER PENNY
## CHEESE COINS

These crispy cheese-cracker coins won't jingle in your pocket, but they'll dance in your mouth! They make a nice party nibble or accompaniment to a bowl of soup.

ACTIVE TIME: 20 MINUTES
TOTAL TIME: 35 MINUTES +
30 MINUTES CHILLING TIME
MAKES ABOUT 40 CHEESE
COINS

- 1 cup shredded sharp Cheddar cheese
- 4 tablespoons butter, softened
- ¾ cup all-purpose flour
- ¼ teaspoon salt
- ¼ teaspoon dry mustard
  Smoked or sweet paprika
  Water, as needed

In a medium bowl, combine the cheese, butter, flour, salt, and mustard. Beat with an electric mixer on medium until a cohesive dough begins to form, sprinkling with a little water if it remains crumbly.

**KIDS CAN HELP!** As soon as the dough starts to come together, gather into a rough ball. Transfer to a lightly floured surface and roll into an 8-inch log about 1½ inches in diameter. Wrap tightly in plastic wrap and chill in the freezer for 30 minutes.

Heat oven to 400°F. Line a large rimmed baking pan with parchment paper. Using a serrated knife, slice the log crosswise into ⅛-inch-thick rounds. Place on the prepared pan with about ½ inch between them. Sprinkle with a little paprika.

Bake until they're just beginning to brown, 12 to 15 minutes. Remove from the oven. Let cool on the pan for 5 to 10 minutes, then transfer to wire racks to cool completely. (Coins will crisp up as they cool.)

**Make a Color Poppin' Plate!** Serve with green and red apple wedges or red grapes.

# CHOCOLATE SPRINKLES
## CHOCOLATE WAFFLES WITH MARSHMALLOW WHIPPED CREAM

It doesn't get more decadent than chocolate waffles studded with chocolate sprinkles and topped with chocolate syrup and marshmallow whipped cream. Is it dessert? Is it breakfast? You choose!

ACTIVE TIME: 40 MINUTES
TOTAL TIME: 40 MINUTES
MAKES 4 TO 6 SERVINGS

### FOR THE WHIPPED CREAM

- 1 cup heavy whipping cream, chilled
- 1 (7-ounce) jar marshmallow fluff
- 1 teaspoon vanilla extract

### FOR THE WAFFLES

- 1½ cups all-purpose flour
- ½ cup sugar
- ¼ cup unsweetened cocoa powder
- 2 teaspoons baking powder
- ½ teaspoon baking soda
- ½ teaspoon salt
- 2 large eggs
- 1 cup whole milk
- 4 tablespoons butter, melted and cooled slightly
- 1 teaspoon vanilla
- 1 tablespoon orange zest
- ¼ cup chocolate sprinkles, plus more for garnish
  Nonstick cooking spray
  Chocolate syrup, for serving

**Make the whipped cream:** In a large bowl, beat the whipping cream with an electric mixer on high until soft peaks form. Add the marshmallow fluff and vanilla, and continue to whip on high, scraping the sides of the bowl occasionally until a loose whipped cream forms. Cover and refrigerate until serving time.

**Make the waffles:** Heat oven to 200°F.

**KIDS CAN HELP!** In a large bowl, whisk together the flour, sugar, cocoa, baking powder, baking soda, and salt. In a medium bowl, whisk together the eggs, milk, butter, vanilla, and orange zest.

**KIDS CAN HELP!** Make a well in the dry ingredients. Add the egg mixture all at once. Stir gently just until combined. Stir in the ¼ cup chocolate sprinkles.

Heat a waffle iron. Spray with nonstick cooking spray. Pour batter onto hot waffle iron and cook until golden brown, 4 to 5 minutes. Keep cooked waffles warm on a baking sheet in the oven.

**KIDS CAN HELP!** To serve, place a waffle on a plate. Drizzle with chocolate syrup. Dollop with whipped cream and sprinkle with additional chocolate sprinkles.

**Make a Color Poppin' Plate!** Serve with pitted and halved sweet cherries or fresh strawberries.

# CINNAMON STICK
## HOT COCOA

Warm up with a steaming mug of homemade hot cocoa after sledding, skating, building a snowman—or just because.

ACTIVE TIME: 10 MINUTES
TOTAL TIME: 20 MINUTES
MAKES 4 SERVINGS

4  cups whole milk

½  cup unsweetened cocoa powder

½  cup brown sugar

½  teaspoon ground cinnamon

Pinch of salt

1  teaspoon vanilla extract

Whipped cream

Chocolate sprinkles

4  cinnamon sticks

In a large saucepan, whisk together the milk, cocoa powder, brown sugar, ground cinnamon, salt, and vanilla. Bring to a boil over medium-high. Reduce heat and simmer for 5 minutes. Whisk vigorously to create froth.

**KIDS CAN HELP!** Divide mixture among 4 mugs. Top with whipped cream and chocolate sprinkles, and insert cinnamon sticks.

# CANVAS ART

Some flowers and words of welcome add a homey touch to your dining room or breakfast nook.

## WHAT YOU NEED

Crayola Signature® Sketch & Detail Dual Ended Markers

Blank canvas

Crayola Signature® Pearlescent Paint Markers

## HOW YOU MAKE IT

Draw a circular floral design with markers on the canvas.

Add outlines and details with paint markers.

Write a message in the center of the flower circle with the chisel tip of a marker.

Trace the bottom half of the message with the fine line tip of the marker.

Blend colors using the chisel tip of the marker to create an ombré effect.

Display your beautiful canvas!

# INDEX

PO Box 3088
San Rafael, CA 94912
www.insighteditions.com

Find us on Facebook: www.facebook.com/InsightEditions
Follow us on Twitter: @insighteditions
Follow us on Instagram: @insighteditions

ISBN: 978-8-88663-172-2

INSIGHT EDITIONS
Publisher: Raoul Goff
VP, Co-Publisher: Vanessa Lopez
VP, Creative: Chrissy Kwasnik
VP, Manufacturing: Alix Nicholaeff
VP, Group Managing Editor: Vicki Jaeger
Publishing Director: Jamie Thompson
Art Director: Stuart Smith
Editor: Joanna Botelho
Editorial Assistant: Jennifer Pellman
Managing Editor: Maria Spano
Senior Production Editor: Katie Rokakis
Production Associate: Deena Hashem
Senior Production Manager, Subsidiary Rights: Lina s Palma-Temena

WATERBURY PUBLICATIONS, INC.
Editorial Director: Lisa Kingsley
Creative Director: Ken Carlson
Associate Art Director: Doug Samuelson
Photographer: Ken Carlson
Food Stylist: Jennifer Peterson
Food Stylist Assistant: Holly Wiederin

Insight Editions, in association with Roots of Peace, will plant two trees for each tree used in the manufacturing of this book. Roots of Peace is an internationally renowned humanitarian organization dedicated to eradicating land mines worldwide and converting war-torn lands into productive farms and wildlife habitats. Roots of Peace will plant two million fruit and nut trees in Afghanistan and provide farmers there with the skills and support necessary for sustainable land use.

Manufactured in China by Insight Editions

10 9 8 7 6 5 4 3 2 1